BRITISH RAILWAYS STEAM HAULED PASSENGER TRAINS IN THE SIXTIES

Volume One

Compiled by
PETER HANDS

DEFIANT PUBLICATIONS
190 Yoxall Road,
Shirley, Solihull,
West Midlands

Printed on behalf of Richard Netherwood Ltd., by Gorenjski tisk p.o., Slovenia

CURRENT STEAM PHOTOGRAPH ALBUMS AVAILABLE
FROM DEFIANT PUBLICATIONS

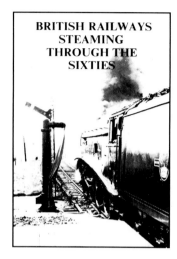

BRITISH RAILWAYS STEAMING THROUGH THE SIXTIES

VOLUME 11
A4 size - Hardback. 100 pages
-180 b/w photographs.
£10.95 + £1.00 postage.
ISBN 0 946857 24 5.

BRITISH RAILWAYS STEAMING THROUGH THE SIXTIES

VOLUME 12
A4 size - Hardback. 100 pages
-182 b/w photographs.
£11.95 + £1.00 postage.
ISBN 0 946857 27 X.

BRITISH RAILWAYS STEAMING THROUGH THE SIXTIES

VOLUME 13
A4 size - Hardback. 100 pages
-182 b/w photographs.
£11.95 + £1.00 postage.
ISBN 0 946857 33 4.

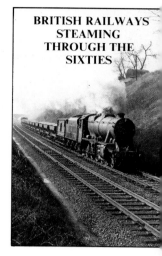

BRITISH RAILWAYS STEAMING THROUGH THE SIXTIES

VOLUME 14
A4 size - Hardback. 96 pages
-178 b/w photographs.
£14.95 + £1.00 postage.
ISBN 0 946857 40 7.

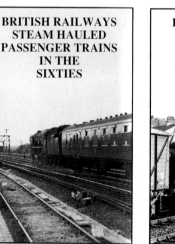

BRITISH RAILWAYS STEAM HAULED PASSENGER TRAINS IN THE SIXTIES

VOLUME 1
A4 size - Hardback. 96 pages
-177 b/w photographs.
£14.95 + £1.00 postage.
ISBN 0 946857 41 5.

BRITISH RAILWAYS STEAM HAULED FREIGHT TRAINS 1948-1968

VOLUME 1
A4 size - Hardback. 96 pages
-174 b/w photographs.
£14.95 + £1.00 postage.
ISBN 0 946857 42 3.

BRITISH RAILWAYS STEAMING THROUGH CREWE, DONCASTER, EASTLEIGH AND SWINDON

IN PREPARATION

BRITISH RAILWAYS STEAMING ON THE SOUTHERN REGION

IN PREPARATION

VOLUME 3

BRITISH RAILWAYS STEAMING ON THE LONDON MIDLAND REGION

VOLUME 3
A4 size - Hardback. 100 pages
-181 b/w photographs.
£11.95 + £1.00 postage.
ISBN 0 946857 28 8.

BRITISH RAILWAYS STEAMING ON THE LONDON MIDLAND REGION

IN PREPARATION

VOLUME 4

BRITISH RAILWAYS STEAMING ON THE EX-LNER LINES

IN PREPARATION

VOLUME 3

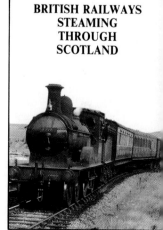

BRITISH RAILWAYS STEAMING THROUGH SCOTLAND

VOLUME 1
A4 size - Hardback. 96 pages
-180 b/w photographs.
£12.95 + £1.00 postage.
ISBN 0 946857 35 0.

CURRENT STEAM PHOTOGRAPH ALBUMS AVAILABLE
FROM DEFIANT PUBLICATIONS

VOLUME 1
A4 size - Hardback. 100 pages
-180 b/w photographs.
£8.95 + £1.00 postage.
ISBN 0 946857 12 1.

VOLUME 2
A4 size - Hardback. 100 pages
-180 b/w photographs.
£8.95 + £1.00 postage.
ISBN 0 946857 13 X.

VOLUME 3
A4 size - Hardback. 100 pages
-180 b/w photographs.
£9.95 + £1.00 postage.
ISBN 0 946857 16 4.

VOLUME 4
A4 size - Hardback. 100 pages
-180 b/w photographs.
£9.95 + £1.00 postage.
ISBN 0 946857 17 2.

VOLUME 5
A4 size - Hardback. 100 pages
-180 b/w photographs.
£9.95 + £1.00 postage.
ISBN 0 946857 22 9.

VOLUME 6
A4 size - Hardback. 100 pages
-180 b/w photographs.
£9.95 + £1.00 postage.
ISBN 0 946857 23 7.

VOLUME 7
OUT OF
PRINT

VOLUME 8
OUT OF
PRINT

VOLUME 9
A4 size - Hardback. 96 pages
-177 b/w photographs.
£14.95 + £1.00 postage.
ISBN 0 946857 37 7.

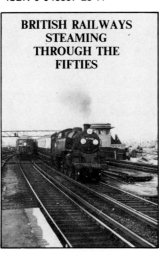

VOLUME 10
A4 size - Hardback. 96 pages
-176 b/w photographs.
£14.95 + £1.00 postage.
ISBN 0 946857 38 5.

VOLUME 1
A4 size - Hardback. 96 pages
-177 b/w photographs.
£14.95 + £1.00 postage.
ISBN 0 946857 39 3.

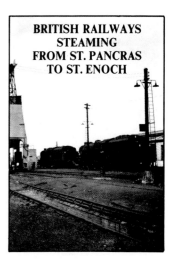

A4 size - Hardback. 96 pages
-173 b/w photographs.
£12.95 + £1.00 postage.
ISBN 0 946857 36 9.

ACKNOWLEDGEMENTS

Grateful thanks are extended to the following contributors of photographs not only for their use in this book but for their kind patience and long term loan of negatives/photographs whilst this book was being compiled.

T.R.AMOS TAMWORTH	P.A.BRIDGMAN HUCCLECOTE	B.W.L.BROOKSBANK LONDON
N.L.BROWNE ALDERSHOT	L.BROWNHILL BRIERLEY HILL	J.K.CARTER MILLHOLME
BRIAN COATES RIVERHEAD, NEW BRUNSWICK, CANADA		D.COLES HIGH WYCOMBE
BARRY J.FLEMING *	D.A.GOODALL CUFFLEY	PETER HAY HOVE
R.W.HINTON GLOUCESTER	H.L.HOLLAND ST.CATHERINES, ONTARIO, CANADA	
F.HORNBY NORTH CHEAM	A.C.INGRAM WISBECH	H.N.JAMES IPSWICH
ALAN JONES BATH	D.K.JONES MOUNTAIN ASH	R.J.LEITCH SAWSTON
DENIS LEWIS TEIGNMOUTH	A.F.NISBET BRACKLEY	D.OAKES HITCHIN
R.PICTON WOLVERHAMPTON	W.POTTER BISHOPS CLEEVE	N.E.PREEDY HUCCLECOTE
J.H.PRICE *	J.SCHATZ LITTLETHORPE	K.L.SEAL ANDOVERSFORD
G.W.SHARPE BARNSLEY	DEREK SINGLETON **	M.S.STOKES MARPLE
J.M.TOLSON ***	MIKE TURNER BROAD HINTON	D.WEBSTER ****
KIT WINDLE LOWER BREDBURY	MIKE WOOD BIRMINGHAM	

*   Courtesy of the Andrew Ingram collection.
**   From the Preston Whiteley collection (Kendall) courtesy of David Alexander.
***   Courtesy of the Frank Hornby collection.
**** Courtesy of the Norman Preedy collection.

Front Cover -Looking somewhat neglected externally, SR Rebuilt *Merchant Navy* Class 4-6-2 No 35007 *Aberdeen Commonwealth*, from 70G Weymouth, passes through Farnborough, between Weybridge and Basingstoke, with an express on 'Whit Saturday', 28th May 1966. (D.Oakes)

ISBN 0 946857 41 5

(C) P.B.HANDS 1993
FIRST PUBLISHED 1993

INTRODUCTION

BRITISH RAILWAYS STEAM HAULED PASSENGER TRAINS IN THE SIXTIES - Volume One is a spin-off from the earlier 'Steaming Through the Sixties' albums and adds another dimension to the overall series of books within the 'BR Steaming' range.

The 'BR Steaming' books are designed to give the ordinary, everyday steam photographic enthusiast of the 1950's and 1960's a chance to participate in and give pleasure to others whilst recapturing the twilight days of steam.

Apart from the 1950's and 1960's series, individual albums will be produced from time to time. Wherever possible no famous names will be found, nor will photographs which have been published before be used, but the content and quality of the majority of photographs used will be second to none.

BRITISH RAILWAYS STEAM HAULED PASSENGER TRAINS IN THE SIXTIES - Volume One is divided into six chapters, each on a regional basis. For the enthusiast of the individual regions there is a wide selection of locomotive classes at work on passenger trains, from the humblest tank engine on local duties to the elite engines employed on the crack expresses of the day.

Unlike the fifties, when almost every passenger train was steam hauled, the sixties were a time of total decline for steam, culminating in the demise of the same in August 1968. Many of the engines seen within the pages of this book are in a state of neglect, but nevertheless the author hopes that the contents will bring back many memories of those far off days.

The continuation of the 'BR Steaming' series etc., depends upon *you* the reader. If you wish to join my direct mailing list for future albums and/or feel you have suitable material of BR steam locomotives between 1948-1968 and wish to contribute them towards this series and other albums, please contact:

Tel. No.
021 745-8421

Peter Hands,
190 Yoxall Road,
Shirley, Solihull,
West Midlands B90 3RN

CONTENTS

CHAPTER ONE - LONDON MIDLAND REGION

1) A raised upper quadrant clears the road ahead for BR *Britannia* Class 4-6-2 No 70054 *Dornoch Firth*, from 2D Banbury, as a spotter peers into the cab prior to the locomotive departing with an express from Nottingham (Victoria) on 16th October 1965. The filthy condition of *Dornoch Firth*, bereft of name and shedplates, belies the fact that it was only eleven years or so old at this stage in time. (D.Webster)

2) Although Crewe was the 'heart and soul' of the LMS former Great Western locomotives were regular visitors on local passenger trains from Wellington during the sixties. Beneath the wires in a bay platform in April 1962 is GWR 5100 Class 2-6-2T No 4178, an inhabitant of 84H Wellington shed since September 1960, seen here working bunker- first in charge of a two coach non corridor suburban train. (Kit Windle)

3) Steam to the rescue, a common event as the earlier diesels had teething troubles for a long time after they were first introduced. BR Class 9F 2-10-0 No 92122, a 15C Leicester (Midland) engine, is seen at rest within the confines of Euston station after arriving with the 1.27pm express from Blackpool on 4th April 1961. Trailing behind No 92122 is a failed 'Peak' Type 4 diesel No D7 *Ingleborough*. (R.W.Hinton)

4) Photographed from the shed yard at 5C Stafford during 1961, LMS *Coronation* Class 4-6-2 No 46246 *City of Manchester*, from 1B Camden, restarts a northbound express out of the station. Constructed at Crewe Works during the dark depths of the Second World War in 1943, *City of Manchester* was streamlined, but in common with others of the class it later resorted to the more conventional shape common to most engines. (D.K.Jones)

5) Years of neglect at Uppingham are shown clearly within this picture with the overgrown trackbed on the left and the rotting station roof to the right. The main focus of the photograph is LMS Class 4F 0-6-0 No 44414, of 15C Leicester (Midland), specially spruced up to take charge of a Railway Correspondence & Travel Society special on 18th May 1963 - 'The East Midlands Railtour'. Uppingham station had been closed in 1960. (D.Webster)

6) Another RCTS inspired special, this time the location is in Merseyside. 17A Derby based LMS Class 4 2-6-4T No 42587 is far from home as it passes Aintree signalbox bunker-first on 27th May 1960. No 42587, sporting express lamps, was transferred to 16A Nottingham in March 1961. After several more transfers within the LMR it finally ended its career on the North Eastern Region, at 56F Low Moor. (D.K.Jones)

7) Most expresses to and from Birmingham (New Street) to Liverpool and Manchester were hauled by LMS *Patriot*, *Royal Scot* and *Jubilee* Classes of 4-6-0's, along with the occasional *Coronation* Pacific. It was always a disappointment when a less famous type was employed as is the case on this unknown day in 1963 when LMS Class 5 4-6-0 No 44863, from 2A Rugby, arrives with a combined Liverpool/Manchester train. (L.Brownhill)

8) Nowadays the name of Newport Pagnell is more associated with the services on the M1 than with railways, but until 1964 it had a station which linked with Wolverton via Great Linford and Bradwell. On a wet and dismal day on 4th April 1964 LMS Class 2 2-6-2T No 41222 steams into Newport Pagnell with the 2.45pm local from Wolverton. Based at 1E Bletchley for many years, No 41222 was moved to Carlisle in 1965. (J.Schatz)

9) Despite the presence of overhead wires steam was still dominant between Crewe and Stafford during the early sixties on all forms of traffic, including express workings. LMS *Royal Scot* Class 4-6-0 No 46144 *Honourable Artillery Company*, allocated to 6G Llandudno Junction, (in filthy external condition), heads a Liverpool to Birmingham express just south of Crewe on the up fast line in August 1962. (Kit Windle)

10) Stanier Pacific power at Preston shortly before the demise of the *Coronation* Class on the West Coast Main Line. LMS Class 8P 4-6-2 No 46251 *City of Nottingham*, of 5A Crewe (North), is passing Preston No. 5 signalbox with a Stephenson Locomotive Society special from Birmingham (New Street) to Carlisle (Citadel) on 12th July 1964, a few short weeks before being taken out of service in October 1964. (H.L.Holland)

11) Weak sunshine filters into Bolton (Trinity Street) station on 3rd May 1965. Excess steam blows gently from the safety valves of' BR Class 4 4-6-0 No 75047, from 8K Bank Hall (Liverpool), which is heading a three coach local passenger. No 75047 remained on Bank Hall's books until February 1966 being drafted to 5D Stoke. Before withdrawal in August 1967 it had spells at Machynlleth, Shrewsbury and Croes Newydd. (B.W.L.Brooksbank)

12) At one time Mansfield boasted three stations - Central (closed in 1956) along with Town and Woodhouse (both closed during 1964). The first belonged to the Great Central with the latter two being Midland Railway orientated. With a shunter keeping a close eye on events, BR Class 9F 2-10-0 No 92155, of 2E Saltley, backs onto an enthusiasts special at Mansfield (Town) on 8th May 1965. (D.Webster)

13) With a town in the righthand distance LMS Class 5 4-6-0 No 44933, an inmate of 9D Newton Heath, comes down the grade and approaches the shed at Lower Darwen with the 2.08pm express from Manchester to Blackburn on 4th September 1964. This train is the successor (from Manchester) of the through service from Euston to Colne which last ran two years earlier in September 1962. (H.L.Holland)

14) Although Great Western in origin Birmingham (Snow Hill) became the property of the London Midland Region during 1962/63. In this picture, taken on 8th August 1964, we are looking southwards where London bound trains disappear into the gloom of the tunnel in the distance. Facing the camera is GWR *Hall* Class 4-6-0 No 6925 *Hackness Hall*, which is in charge of the 1.11pm Portsmouth to Wolverhampton express. (B.W.L.Brooksbank)

15) Might and majesty at Preston station on 10th October 1963. LMS *Coronation* Class 4-6-2 No 46245 *City of London*, from 1A Willesden, graces the station with an unidentified express, shortly after being ousted from 1B Camden by diesel power. During its railway history Preston had a number of other stations - Deepdale, Maudland Bridge, Maudlands, Maxwell House and Oxheys - all closing between 1844 and 1930. (D.K.Jones)

16) In charge of the 7.50am from Sheffield (Midland) on 2nd August 1964, LNER Thompson Bl Class 4-6-0 No 61094, allocated to 41D Canklow, glides past an elevated signalbox as it approaches Manchester (Central) station. By this stage in time the Hope Valley route was not a serious contender for inter-city traffic, which was concentrated on the ex. GCR electrified route from Manchester (Piccadilly) to Sheffield (Victoria). (H.L.Holland)

17) Photographers lean out of the leading carriage of a northbound express, which is being hauled by an unidentified LMS Class 5 4-6-0 on the outskirts of Carlisle, to record the passing of BR *Britannia* Class 4-6-2 No 70002 *Geoffrey Chaucer*, from 12A Carlisle (Kingmoor), as it heads south with an up express on 4th July 1964. *Geoffrey Chaucer* had been an inmate of Kingmoor since a transfer from 31B March in December 1963. (D.K.Jones)

18) LMS *Royal Scot* Class 4-6-0 No 46131 *The Royal Warwickshire Regiment*, a 6G Llandudno Junction steed, rushes through a deserted Queens Ferry station on upgraded track with a Euston to Holyhead express in August 1962. The shed staff at Llandudno Junction certainly had not expended any energy in keeping *The Royal Warwickshire Regiment* clean. Perhaps they already knew it was marked for withdrawal two months later? (Kit Windle)

19) 1962 was the last year of service for the magnificent LMS Stanier *Princess* Class 4-6-2's, or what was left of them. Half of their ranks had been condemned during 1961, leaving Nos 46200/1/3/6/8/9 to soldier on. On 7th August 1962 No 46203 *Princess Margaret Rose*, from 12A Carlisle (Kingmoor), gets the 8.45am Euston to Wolverhampton (High Level) express on the move as it climbs the grade at Birmingham (New Street) (J.Schatz)

20) With a member of the footplate crew leaning out of the cab of his charge, BR *Britannia* Class 4-6-2 No 70031 *Byron*, a resident of 9A Longsight (Manchester), blackens the skyline at Cheadle Heath as it charges through the station with an express in May 1961. Three months later and *Byron* was to be found at a new home - 21D Aston, where it remained until April 1963, moving on to 1A Willesden. (R.W.Hinton)

21) High summer on the Settle and Carlisle near Kirkby Stephen where the wildflowers on the embankment in the left of the picture are magnificent, especially the Cowslips. The peace and tranquility of the area is disturbed momentarily as LMS *Jubilee* Class 4-6-0 No 45568 *Western Australia*, from 55A Leeds (Holbeck), bursts out of a tunnel and roars towards the camera with a holiday express on 27th July 1960. (Derek Singleton)

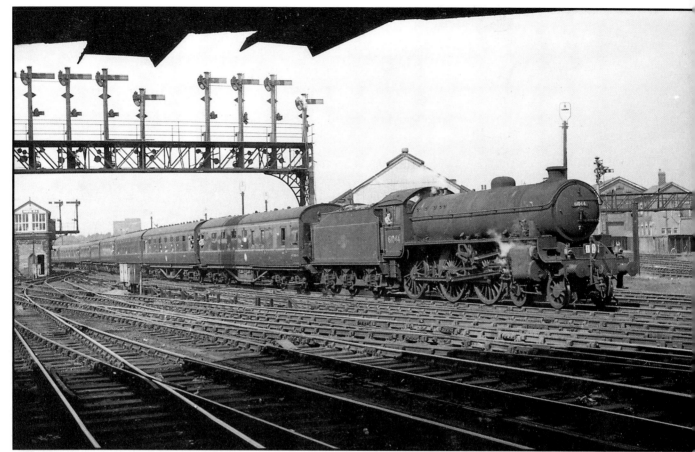

22) A splendid view of the western approaches to Chester (General) with a magnificent array of LNWR signals dominating the skyline. During the hectic summer months on the North Wales main line all types of locomotives were employed on holiday expresses, as is the case with this Llandudno to Wakefield extra in August 1963. In charge of this express is 41D Canklow based LNER Thompson Bl Class 4-6-0 No 61044. (Kit Windle)

23) A quaint scene at Marylebone station on 20th April 1963 with an unusual set of lower quadrant signals, ornate lighting and elderly road goods vehicles in view. In charge of a local passenger train is LMS Class 4 2-6-4T No 42178, from 2F Woodford Halse. Once of 14B Kentish Town No 42178 had been drafted to 14D Neasden in February 1960 and thence to Woodford where it was condemned in July 1963. (A.F.Nisbet)

24) Multiple trackwork, a modern signalbox, gas holders and a tall factory chimney fill the camera lens at Wigan on 3rd September 1964. British Railways built LMS inspired Caprotti Class 5 4-6-0 No 44756, of 8M Southport, is passing alongside the West Coast Main Line with the 1.07pm Manchester to Southport stopping train. The loco is only a matter of days away from withdrawal from 8M. (H.L.Holland)

25) Another LMS Class 5 4-6-0 (in more conventional form) No 45070, from 8F Springs Branch Wigan, heads a down extra at full speed through Tebay station on 30th March 1964, its driver having dismissed from his mind the possibility of summoning banking assistance over Shap. Tebay station, closed in 1968, consisted of a hotch-potch of buildings, offering scant protection to would be travellers. 'Bleak House' is rather apt!! (H.L.Holland)

26) A busy steam-filled scene at Rugby (Midland) in August 1962. In immaculate external condition LMS *Coronation* Class 4-6-2 No 46235 *City of Birmingham*, a longstanding inmate of 5A Crewe (North), blows off steam prior to setting off with an express. In the right of the picture LMS *Princess* Class 4-6-2 No 46206 *Princess Marie Louise*, from 1B Camden, waits for its path to be cleared with a parcels train. (D.K.Jones)

27) Bleak moorlands provide a backdrop to the remote area within the vicinity of Scout Green, on the formidable Shap incline, an inhospitable area of England during all but a few months of the year. On 21st June 1961, LMS Class 5 4-6-0 No 44715, a 2A Rugby engine, powers an express past the camera. Having been based at Rugby for many years, No 44715 was ousted in May 1965, moving to 5B Crewe (South). (D.K.Jones)

28) LMS Hughes 'Crab' Class 6P5F 2-6-0 No 42942 (8H Birkenhead) is temporarily detached from its coaches whilst on special duty at Denbigh on 24th September 1966. No 42942 is being employed on the Locomotive Club of Great Britain 'Conway Valley Railtour'. Denbigh station, closed in 1962, was situated on the route from Rhyl which eventually wound its way to Aberystwyth by way of Corwen and Bala. (N.E.Preedy)

29) Western Region locomotives were a common sight at Chester entering the station by way of the former Great Western main line from Shrewsbury. GWR *Grange* Class 4-6-0 No 6879 *Overton Grange*, an 84E Tyseley engine, drifts into Chester (General) with a summer extra from Cardiff to Birkenhead on 22nd July 1961. To the left of *Overton Grange* is LMS Class 4 2-6-4T No 42606, from 6C Birkenhead. (B.W.L.Brooksbank)

30) Complicated pointwork litters the approaches to Spalding station in Lincolnshire on 25th August 1962 as LNER Gresley K3 Class 2-6-0 No 61817, from 31B March, arrives with an express. (Note the sectioned crossing barriers in the right of the frame.) No 61817 may well have been performing one of its last passenger duties for it was condemned the following month, being cut up at the Central Wagon Co., Ince, Wigan in December 1963. (T.R.Amos)

31) Apart from the Pullman car in the right background the locomotive and carriages in the foreground at Hornsey are of Gresley vintage. LNER A3 Class 4-6-2 No 60046 *Diamond Jubilee*, allocated to 34F Grantham, heads northbound with a down express in August 1961. Built in 1924, *Diamond Jubilee* was originally given the number 2545. Modified with a double chimney in July 1958, it later received German smoke deflectors. (N.E.Preedy)

32) More Pacific power on the East Coast Main Line this time in the shape of Peppercorn LNER A1 Class 4-6-2 No 60117 *Bois Roussel* (built by British Railways in 1948). *Bois Roussel* is in charge of an unidentified southbound express on Sunday 29th December 1963 at Barkston South Junction. Allocated to 56C Copley Hill, No 60117 was transferred to 56B Ardsley upon the closure of the former in September 1964. (K.L.Seal)

33) The Great Eastern Railway spared no expense when it constructed the roof at March station, providing its customers with more than adequate shelter from the elements. Awaiting departure from March on an August day in 1960 is locally based LNER K3 Class 2-6-0 No 61810. Surplus to requirements at 31B in December 1960 No 61810 moved on briefly to 40A Lincoln. It ended its days at 34E New England. (N.E.Preedy)

34) Far from its home at Blackpool LMS Class 5 4-6-0 No 44737 finds itself in alien territory at Doncaster station on 5th August 1962. No 44737 takes on fresh water supplies on a through road whilst in charge of an excursion. After the closure of the main shed at Blackpool in September 1964, No 44737 found a new lease of life at 9K Bolton. It served from Bank Hall and Springs Branch Wigan prior to withdrawal in 1967. (J.Schatz)

35) Enthusiasts of both sexes and of all ages and shapes and sizes throng the overbridge and platforms at Thetford, in Norfolk on 3rd March 1962. The occasion is a railtour with two smartly turned out locomotives in view. Carrying express headlamps is 31B March based BR *Britannia* Class 4-6-2 No 70003 *John Bunyan*, which is in the company of veteran former Great Eastern Railway J17 Class 0-6-0 No 65567 (32A Norwich). (D.Webster)

36) Much has changed over the thirty-one years since this picture was taken in April 1962 with the forms of traction utilised to and from Kings Cross. Steam was superseded by diesels and now overhead wires clutter the cramped confines. LNER A3 Class 4-6-2 No 60059 *Tracery* (34A Kings Cross) is seen in its final form with a double chimney and German smoke deflectors as it arrives with the up *Yorkshire Pullman*. (N.E.Preedy)

37) Heavily laden trees bow to the passing of 50A York based LNER V2 Class 2-6-2 No 60837 (with a partially scorched smokebox) as it powers an East Coast Main Line express near to Markham, between Tuxford North and Retford on 2nd September 1961. From January 1957, No 60837 spent most of its working life at York, the exception being a spell at 56C Copley Hill, between June and October 1959. (D.K.Jones)

38) Signals a'plenty at Peterborough (North) on a grey day on 6th August 1960. A filthy looking LNER K3 Class 2-6-0 No 61948, one of the fleet allocated to 31B March, passes the small signalbox at the north end of the station with its load of three coaches (one being of Gresley origin) and two wagons which form a stopping train from the Grimsby line. No 61948 survived in service at 31B until March 1962. (F.Hornby)

39) More Pacific power on show at Kings Cross terminus with another LNER A3 Class 4-6-2 in its final form. Looking fresh from workshops locally based No 60061 *Pretty Polly* has been rostered at 34A to take charge of an express to Newcastle in March 1962. It was equipped with a double chimney in October 1958 and further modified with the German style deflectors in February 1962. (N.E.Preedy)

40) Nearing the end of its days as a 34A Kings Cross locomotive, LNER A4 Class 4-6-2 No 60021 *Wild Swan*, in begrimed condition, steams through Hitchin northbound, with a down express on 1st April 1963. Ousted from 34A in June 1963 *Wild Swan* trekked northwards to a new home at 34E New England where it was little used until condemnation in October of the same year. It was scrapped at Doncaster in January 1964. (D.Oakes)

41) A passenger train has just negotiated the points at a junction near March on 11th August 1962, as BR Class 4 4-6-0 No 75042, from 15C Leicester (Midland), approaches the same, under clear signals, with an unidentified express on 11th August 1962. As the diesels tightened their grip in East Anglia scenes like this were soon to become nothing more than a memory, with steam disappearing from March in December 1963. (T.R.Amos)

42) Various goods wagons occupy sidings in and around the vicinity of Sleaford station on 6th July 1963. The centrepiece of this photograph is of the much celebrated and nowadays actively preserved LNER A4 Class 4-6-2 No 60007 *Sir Nigel Gresley*, newly allocated to 34E New England from 34A Kings Cross. *Sir Nigel Gresley* has paused for refreshment whilst in charge of the LCGB 'Mallard Commemorative Rail Tour'. (D.Webster)

43) The crossing gates have clanged shut and the signals set for the passing of a train through the sleepy station at Rauceby, near Sleaford on 27th July 1963. Before too long the rails begin to hum as the sight and sounds of a steam hauled express approaches. Exhaust steam trails behind LNER Bl Class 4-6-0 No 61264, from 40E Colwick, as it blasts through with the 1.23pm from Skegness to Leicester. (N.E.Preedy)

44) A four coach local consisting of a mixture of stock, hauled by unkempt looking LMS 'Flying Pig' Class 4 2-6-0 No 43010, of 15A Wellingborough, passes Peterborough (North) station on its way to Peterborough (East) on 6th August 1960. No 43010's load is a through train from the Midlands to East Anglia. This locomotive's run of the mill career was brought to an end from 12D Workington in December 1967. (N.L.Browne)

45) More special traffic, this time at Peterborough (East). A smartly turned out LMS *Royal Scot* Class 4-6-0 No 46155 *The Lancer*, from 5A Crewe (North), clears its cylinder cocks whilst at the head of the LCGB 'Pennine Limited' on 19th September 1964. The following month *The Lancer* was drafted to 12A Carlisle (Kingmoor), but it was condemned two months later and scrapped at the West of Scotland Shipbreaking Co., Troon. (F.Hornby)

46) LNER V2 Class 2-6-2 No 60871, from the 'Top Shed' at 34A Kings Cross, shows its paces as it climbs the 1 in 200 gradient on the approach to the 987 yard long Peascliffe Tunnel, a short distance to the north of Grantham on 25th August 1962. No 60871 is in charge of a Kings Cross to Newcastle relief. Before withdrawal in September 1963, No 60871 had two further homes - 34E New England and 36A Doncaster. (T.R.Amos)

47) A lone railwayman glances round as 40B Immingham based BR *Britannia* Class 4-6-2 No 70039 *Sir Christopher Wren* takes its leave of Kings Cross station with the 4.12pm express to Cleethorpes on a March day in 1963. Once of 30A Stratford and 32A Norwich, *Sir Christopher Wren* took its leave of the Great Eastern section of the Eastern Region in November 1960 when it joined a number of sister engines at 40B. (A.F.Nisbet)

48) As can be seen in the previous picture the shed staff at Immingham took great care to keep its *Britannia's* up to scratch in terms of cleanliness, which is more than can be said about the condition of this example from its stud of LNER B1 Class 4-6-0's No 61190 heads the 'Butlins Express', which originated from Skegness. The cleanest item on this locomotive is the headboard as it arrives at Peterborough on 6th August 1960. (F.Hornby)

49) The once common sight of tank locomotives hauling local passenger workings up and down the East Coast Main Line from Kings Cross was soon to become a thing of the past as diesel multiple units and diesel engines invaded the area in the late fifties and early sixties. Former GNR N7/3 Class 0-6-2T No 69696 (34C Hatfield) nears its home whilst running tender-first with an up Dunstable train on 19th August 1960. (Barry J.Fleming)

50) The railway outpost at Norwich officially lost its steam allocation from the shed at 32A during March 1962, but continued to service steam until September of that year. On 22nd April 1961 steam was still in command of most expresses to and from London's Liverpool Street station as can be seen in this photo of BR *Britannia* Class 4-6-2 No 70013 *Oliver Cromwell* as it departs from Norwich with such a service. (T.R.Amos)

51) Smoke and steam from the double blastpipes of two Gresley Pacifics invade the atmosphere at King Cross terminus on a bright, sunny day in May 1962. In charge of two down expresses are LNER A4 Class 4-6-2 No 60034 *Lord Faringdon* (34A Kings Cross) and LNER A3 Class 4-6-2 No 60036 *Colombo* (56B Ardsley). Mixed fortunes lay ahead for these locos, No 60036 being withdrawn in November 1964 and 60034 in August 1966. (N.E.Preedy)

52) Most enthusiasts specials were brought about either to commemorate some momentous happening or to mourn a line closing/farewell to steam etc. This photograph taken at Skegness on 24th April 1965 may well fall into the latter category. Hordes of spotters are gathered within the vicinity of LMS Ivatt 'Flying Pig' Class 4 2-6-0 No 43108, from 41D Canklow, which heads an LCGB inspired railtour. (D.Webster)

53) A wet and dismal autumn day at Brookmans Park, between Potters Bar and Hatfield, near to the border of Middlesex and Hertfordshire in 1962. The photographer records the passing of LNER A4 Class 4-6-2 No 60033 *Seagull*, from 34A Kings Cross, as it speeds by with an unidentified express. Vintage 1938, *Seagull* was one of the first A4 Pacifics to be taken out of traffic, from Kings Cross in December 1962. (D.K.Jones)

54) We take a final look at Peterborough (North) station, where, under clear signals, a bedraggled looking LNER A3 Class 4-6-2 No 60050 *Persimmon*, allocated to 34F Grantham and equipped with a double chimney (April 1959), heads an up express bound for Kings Cross on 6th August 1960. *Persimmon* acquired German smoke deflectors in October 1961, some twenty months before withdrawal in June 1963 from 34E New England. (F.Hornby)

55) By the latter part of 1961 the majority of BR *Britannia* Class 4-6-2's based at 32A Norwich had succumbed to the advancing legions of main line diesels and surrendered their turns on the Liverpool Street to Norwich expresses. No 70003 *John Bunyan*, by now a 31B March engine, returns to its old haunt at Liverpool Street, courtesy of the RCTS organised 'Great Eastern Tour' on 31st March 1962. (D.Webster)

56) On the LNER B1 Class 4-6-0's the numberplate was situated between the hinges on the smokebox door, but in this photograph of No 61024 *Addax*, from 56A Wakefield, there is not enough room. The numberplate has been re-located in a higher position. *Addax* is seen on an excursion at Doncaster on 5th August 1962. Transferred to 56B Ardsley in December 1962, No 61024 returned once more to Wakefield in March 1963. (J.Schatz)

57) Once it was announced that 34A Kings Cross was to close on 17th June 1963, some of the charges in their care were neglected by the shed staff. This is the condition that LNER A4 Class 4-6-2 No 60008 *Dwight D.Eisenhower* was in when it was transferred to 34E New England after the demise of 34A. On 23rd June 1963 it is photographed in action near St.Neots on an express. It was withdrawn the following month. (R.J.Leitch)

58) Exhaust steam drifts beneath a canopy at Wood Green station from the chimney of LNER A1 Class 4-6-2 No 60157 *Great Eastern*, from 36A Doncaster, as it beats a path northwards with a down East Coast Main Line express on 4th November 1960. Designed by Peppercorn, *Great Eastern* was constructed during 1949 and was one of five members of the class which were fitted with roller bearings throughout. (T.R.Amos)

59) This is a final view of steam in action during its death throes on the ECML, between Kings Cross and Peterborough. Taken from a goods yard at Hitchin we catch a glimpse of 55H Leeds (Neville Hill) based LNER A3 Class 4-6-2 No 60070 *Gladiateur* which is in charge of a down express on 12th May 1963. Transferred to 52A Gateshead in December 1963 it proved to be the final home for No 60070, withdrawn in May 1964. (D.Oakes)

60) We take our leave of the Eastern Region section with this photograph of LNER BI Class 4-6-0 No 61225, based locally at 36E, which is leaking steam whilst standing in Retford station on the ECML on 21st May 1964. No 61225 is about to depart with the Sheffield portion of the down 'West Riding' express, a rather grandiose title for a train consisting of just three coaches and a parcels type van. (K.L.Seal)

61) We commence the North Eastern chapter with a photograph of an enthusiasts special organised jointly by the Railway Correspondence & Travel Society and the Stephenson Locomotive Society on 28th September 1963. In command of the train is LNER BI Class 4-6-0 No 61037 *Jairou* (51A Darlington) which steams out of Bishops Auckland station and passes the dilapidated East signalbox with the 'North Eastern Tour'. (N.E.Preedy)

62) Although the *Anglo-Scottish Car Carrier* ran for a number of years on the East Coast Main Line there appears to be a shortage of photographs of the same. On a gloomy summer's day in 1961, LNER A4 Class 4-6-2 No 60026 *Miles Beevor*, one of nineteen members of the class allocated to 34A Kings Cross at this stage in time, speeds through York with the northbound 'Car Carrier'. (Kit Windle)

63) As a continuation to the picture on Page 36 we find the RCTS-SLS 'North Eastern Tour' special at West Auckland, presumably on the same day. The driver of a highly presentable LMS Class 4 2-6-4T No 42405, from 51A Darlington, eases his charge onto the leading carriage of the train under the watchful eyes of his fireman. The weeds in the left of the picture had grown since the closure of the station in 1962. (D.Webster)

64) Although only three months away from condemnation, 34F Grantham based LNER A3 Class 4-6-2 No 60064 *Tagalie* has been rostered from either 52A Gateshead or 52B Heaton to take charge of an Edinburgh (Waverley) to Kings Cross express at Newcastle (Central) in June 1961. It is seen here backing onto the train. Although equipped with a double chimney it never carried German style deflectors. (N.E.Preedy)

65) The photographer takes advantage of the run-down platform at York (Holgate), once used for racetrack clientele, on a bright and sunny 19th May 1964. There must have been a shortage of motive power on this day for the authorities to press into service a Stanier LMS freight engine on a passenger train. Class 8F 2-8-0 No 48703, from 55B Stourton, heads towards York station with a special empty stock working. (H.L.Holland)

6) With his style of dress the character in the right foreground looks more like a person associated with the film 'The Thirty-Nine Steps' than a bona-fida railwayman! Both he and his companion are standing well back as LNER Thompson B1 Class 4-6-0 No 61328, from 40B Immingham, powers an express out of Leeds on a murky day in 1961. No 61328 was destined to spend the rest of its days at Immingham prior to withdrawal. (G.W.Sharpe)

57) Rows of regimented terraced houses look down upon the railway scene at Fitzwilliam on 19th August 1966 as 55A Leeds (Holbeck) Class 5 4-6-0 No 45075, in a shocking external state, is pressed into service with the three coach 16.45 hrs local from Leeds (Central) to Doncaster. As steam had finished from Doncaster shed on 26th June 1966 one can only assume that No 45075 was deputising for a more modern mode of transport. (H.S.Stokes)

68) With the 'folly' style of clocktower lurking in the background, LNER BI Class 4-6-0 No 61379 *Mayflower*, a 40B Immingham engine, departs from Wakefield (Westgate) with a Leeds (Central) to Grimsby express in the early summer of 1962. Note the plaque above the cabside number which refers to the exploits of 'The Pilgrim Fathers' in the original 'Mayflower'. No 61379 was withdrawn in August 1962. (P.A.Bridgman)

69) Far from their normal havens on the Southern and London Midland Regions this unique combination finds itself at York on 13th May 1962. SR *Schools* Class 4-4-0 No 30925 *Cheltenham* (70D Basingstoke) is paired with LMS Class 2P 4-4-0 No 40646 (21B Bescot) at the head of the RCTS 'The East Midlander'. For No 40646, it may well have been its last outing as it was withdrawn this same month. (G.W.Sharpe)

0) The magnificence of the huge overall roof at Newcastle (Central) is evident in this view of the station - circa 1965. One of the last surviving LNER A3 Class 4-6-2's, No 60052 *Prince Palatine*, in inhabitant of 64A St.Margarets (Edinburgh), is employed on an enthusiasts special. Seen here in final BR form, including the yellow stripe on the cab, No 60052 soldiered on at 64A until condemned in January 1966. (N.E.Preedy)

1) A small schoolboy scuttles along the track at Hawes as a photographer (presumably his father) prepares to take a picture. In the background is LNER B16/2 Class 4-6-0 No 61435, allocated to 50B Hull (Dairycoates), which is in charge of an excursion on 25th April 1964. No 61435, a Gresley rebuild from an earlier Raven design, was taken out of revenue earning service three months after this picture was taken. (D.K.Jones)

72) Steam workings in and around the Leeds area was soon to become nothing more than a fond memory for many years (until the preservation movement became more organised) within a few days of this photograph being taken in September 1967. LMS Class 4 2-6-4T No 42616, of 56F Low Moor, departs from Leeds with the Bradford portion of an express. Withdrawn in October 1967, No 42616 was cut up by Drapers, Hull. (Mike Turner)

73) Sunlight and shadows near Darlington in August 1962. 1934 built, Gresley inspired LNER A3 Class 4-6-2 No 60038 *Firdaussi*, from 55A Leeds (Holbeck), heads towards home with an express from Newcastle via the coast route. Equipped with a double chimney, in August 1959, *Firdaussi* was destined never to have German style deflectors despite remaining in service until November 1963. 55H Neville Hill was its last home. (N.E.Preedy)

4) Steam issues from the cylinder cocks of LNER B1 Class 4-6-0 No 61013 *Topi*, a 56B Ardsley locomotive, as it awaits departure from Filey station with a return special to the West Riding of Yorkshire in July 1961. As there are two stations at Filey, including the 'Holiday Camp' (Butlins) the bulk of passengers for this train could well be from the latter location, a popular venue for a family holiday. (Kit Windle)

5) The damp and cold conditions at Bradford on an undesignated day in 1965 help to enhance the steam issuing from both of the locomotives on view. Begrimed LMS Class 5 4-6-0 No 45219, from 55D Royston, sets off with an excursion (1X04) and passes a 'Bo-Bo' Type 2 diesel which is being employed on a local passenger. Transferred to 55A Leeds (Holbeck) in June 1966, No 45219 survived until October 1967. (D.K.Jones)

76) A less than clean LNER Thompson B1 Class 4-6-0 No 61083, of 41C Millhouses, speeds through York station on a centre road and heads southwards with a non-stop express on 29th August 1961. No 61083 had been reallocated to 41C during this same month from 41F Mexborough. It had a final move in January 1962 to 41D Canklow from whence it was withdrawn in September 1963. It was scrapped in April 1964. (D.K.Jones)

77) A final view of the RCTS-LCGB combined 'North Eastern Tour'. This time the train is at Bedlington on the Ashington to Monkseaton line. With its passengers having been disgorged from the train LMS Class 4 2-6-0 No 43057, from 51A Darlington, takes a rest on 29th September 1963. Despite its well maintained look the station was to fall under the 'Beeching Axe' and it was closed during 1964. (N.E.Preedy)

8) Looking in fine fettle 52A Gateshead based LNER A3 Class 4-6-2 No 60040 *Cameronian*, constructed at Doncaster Works in 1934, speeds along with an express at Hart (closed in 1953) near Hartlepool in 1961. *Cameronian* spent the last years of its working life based at sheds in the North Eastern Region, finally succumbing to the inevitable during July 1964. Hughes Bolckows, North Blyth claimed the remains. (N.E.Preedy)

9) There is an element of 'over-kill' in terms of weighing up the combined output of two powerful steam locomotives against their load of just four carriages which is designated as an express by the headlamps carried on the leading engine. LNER V2 Class 2-6-2 No 60921, from 36A Doncaster, pilots LNER Bl Class 4-6-0 No 61276, of 50A York, on the racing ground to the North of York during the summer of 1960. (G.W.Sharpe)

80) For many years a favourite of the shed staff at 55A Leeds (Holbeck), LMS *Jubilee* Class 4-6-0 No 45565 *Victoria* was rendered surplus to requirements and apart from a short spell at 56A Wakefield (February-June 1965) it spent the remainder of its working life from 56F Low Moor shed, withdrawn in January 1967. *Victoria* is at Leeds (Central) in August 1966 with a Saturday's Only express to Blackpool. (D.A.Goodall)

81) A tall, gaunt chimney dominates the skyline at Manningham station which is deep in shadow on 31st May 1961. A smoke and soot-stained LMS Stanier Class 5 4-6-0 No 45330 approaches Manningham with an unidentified express. Resident to 12A Carlisle (Kingmoor), No 45330 was drafted to 27B Aintree in May 1963. The station it is passing through was denuded of its passengers when it closed during 1965. (D.K.Jones)

2) A famous location, a named train and a celebrated locomotive meet up on the East Coast Main Line. The location is the cavernous interior of York and the train is the down *Norseman* from Kings Cross. A small group of youngsters admire the graceful lines of one of the ultimate Gresley masterpieces in the shape of LNER A3 Class 4-6-0 No 60103 *Flying Scotsman*, from 34A Kings Cross, photographed circa 1961. (Denis Lewis)

33) As a direct contrast to the immaculate external condition of *Flying Scotsman* in the previous picture, LNER A2 Class 4-6-2 No 60538 *Velocity*, an inmate of 52B Heaton, is in an unkempt state as it passes the camera near Hartlepool with a York to Newcastle express in July 1960. Built in 1948, *Velocity* had a short working life of only some fourteen years, being condemned from its last home at 52D Tweedmouth in October 1962. (N.E.Preedy)

CHAPTER FOUR - SCOTTISH REGION

84) A small boy watches in awe as a neglected looking LMS *Jubilee* Class 4-6-0 No 45629 *Straits Settlements*, from 12A Carlisle (Kingmoor), prepares to depart from Perth with the up 'West Coast Postal' on 30th July 1964. Although not withdrawn until May 1965 *Straits Settlements* was laid up in store from November 1964. It was eventually sent to Motherwell Machinery & Scrap Co., Wishaw for cutting up. (N.E.Preedy)

5) Deputising for a failed diesel LNER V2 Class 2-6-2 No 60865, allocated to 52A Gateshead, passes some modern units as it tracks towards its destination at Edinburgh (Waverley) between the two shed structures at 64A St.Margarets. No 60865 is in charge of an express from Newcastle in August 1964. Condemned in June 1965 it lay in store at 52B Heaton until October of that year before being despatched for scrapping,. (D.K.Jones)

36) 63A Perth based BR Class 5 4-6-0 No 73005 stands beneath an impressive signal gantry at Stirling with an unidentified express on 18th August 1962. At its zenith Stirling boasted three stations - the main line one which is open today (Caledonian Railway), Stirling Central (Caledonian Railway) and Stirling East (North British Railway). The latter two stations were axed during 1966 thanks to Doctor Beeching. (J.Schatz)

87) Overhead wires and colour light signals at Glasgow (Central) on a grey day in 1963. LMS Class 4 2-6-4T No 42266 (66D Greenock) glides past the old bridge over the Clyde and arrives at the massive terminus with an express from Greenock. Despite being in a condition which could have been a prelude to withdrawal, No 42266 was destined to remain in service at Greenock until March 1966. (A.C.Ingram)

88) A fine view of the London end of Edinburgh (Waverley) station on 8th June 1961. A group of Edinburgh's citizens relax on a bowling green in the right of this picture as LNER A4 Class 4-6-2 No 60004 *William Whitelaw* (64B Haymarket) gets a southbound train on the move. It is about to plunge into Calton Tunnel, beneath Edinburgh Prison, on a downgrade of one in seventy-eight towards Portobello. (D.K.Jones)

89) The platform is clean and tidy (a feature of most Scottish stations) and the flower bed along with the shaped hedge are well maintained by the staff at Gleneagles on 15th June 1960. The station sign proudly informs us that we can change here for Crieff and Comrie. In the platform is former Caledonian Railway Class 3P 4-4-0 No 54485 (63A Perth) on an SLS/RCTS special bound for Crieff. (F.Hornby)

90) Both of the footplate crew enjoy the evening sunshine as their charge arrives with a commuter service at Newport-on-Tay East on 28th August 1963. BR Class 4 2-6-4T No 80090, from 62B Dundee Tay Bridge, has been entrusted with the 6.27pm from Dundee to Tayport. In the left of the picture a section of the platform is constructed from wooden planking together with a hotch-potch of slabs. (A.F.Nisbet)

91) Despite the presence of a few weeds there is little to suggest in this picture, taken on 16th June 1960, that the small terminus at Alyth Town station had been closed for some seven years. A scattering of passengers meander along the tracks and platform after alighting from the SLS/RCTS 'Scottish Railtour' special which is being, hauled by ex. Caledonian Railway Class 2F 0-6-0 No 57441, of 63A Perth. (F.Hornby)

92) We move along two years in time and discover another special organised jointly by the SLS/RCTS. The location is Fairlie Pier (GSWR Section) where LMS Class 4 2-6-4T No 42196 (67C Ayr) is in charge of the tour train on 22nd June 1962 (note the two Caledonian coaches next to the engine). No 42196 moved south of the border to England in October 1963, finding a new home at 55H Leeds (Neville Hill). (F.Hornby)

93) We complete this trio of pictures of special SLS/RCTS traffic with this photograph of the tiny station at Loch Tay where the television aerial on the roof of the building is almost as large as the structure itself. A gaggle of enthusiasts scuttle into the station where we find BR Class 4 2-6-4T No 80092 (63A Perth) at the head of the train on 18th June 1962. Loch Tay station closed in 1935. (F.Hornby)

94) Dwellings of various descriptions litter the landscape at Saltcoats as LNER B1 Class 4-6-0 No 61342, from 65A Eastfield (Glasgow), threads a path between the esplanade and the sea with a Saturday's Only express from Glasgow to Largs on 15th June 1963. No 61342, of longstanding association with 65A Eastfield, was drafted to 66B Motherwell in November 1966, but the staff were not impressed and it was withdrawn the following month. (D.K.Jones)

95) Looking in almost mint condition 64B Haymarket based LNER A3 Class 4-6-2 No 60057 *Ormonde* is photographed near Haymarket in October 1961 with the empty stock of a special passenger train. Seen in final form with a double chimney (October 1958) and German style smoke deflectors (September 1961), *Ormonde* (once a regular inmate of 64B) was in its final spell at the shed, departing at year's end. (N.E.Preedy)

96) Passengers and staff alike throng the platform at Carstairs on 3rd June 1965. Facing the camera is an inhabitant of 64C Dalry Road, LMS Class 5 4-6-0 No 45483, which is in charge of the Edinburgh portion of a Birmingham (New Street) express. In September 1965 No 45483 was transferred to 64A St.Margarets, being condemned in December 1966. Before being scrapped it was stored for nigh on eleven months. (D.Webster)

97) A raised upper quadrant clears the path for a northbound train at Coupar Angus station on 9th June 1965. A soon to be condemned BR Class 5 4-6-0 No 73008, from 61B Ferryhill (Aberdeen), draws into Coupar Angus with the 17.30 hrs Aberdeen to Perth stopping train. Withdrawn three months after this picture was taken No 73008 was sent to Motherwell Machinery & Scrap Co., Wishaw for execution in December 1965. (K.L.Seal)

98) There is a heavy veil of mist hanging over the hills at Callander where we espy the 'old and the new order' on show in the station on 30th March 1964. In the background stabled in a siding is a diesel multiple unit whilst pride of place goes to BR Class 4 2-6-4T No 80061, from 65J Stirling and in immaculate condition, which is in charge of a branch passenger train. Closure for Callander station came in 1965. (D.K.Jones)

99) Cold, wintry and dangerous conditions for would be passengers at the London end of Perth station on Saturday 13th November 1965. Two characters brave the elements and the hazards of the slush-covered platform as LNER A4 Class 4-6-2 No 60034 *Lord Faringdon*, of 61B Ferryhill (Aberdeen), steam and sizzles prior to departing from Perth with an Aberdeen to Glasgow (Buchanan Street) express. (J.H.Price)

100) Another view of Perth (General) and despite it being high summer it is a wet and dismal day. Wet rails glisten as LNER Thompson B1 Class 4-6-0 No 61277, from 62B Dundee Tay Bridge, heads the stock of an empty passenger train beneath a road bridge on 11th August 1963. Once of 65A Eastfield (Glasgow), No 61277 was drafted to the Fife area in May 1957 firstly to 62A Thornton Junction and then to Dundee. (D.K.Jones)

01) The lengthy curving platform at Wemyss Bay is well protected by the sweeping roof as thoughtfully provided by the Caledonian Railway in years gone by. In the platform on 2nd June 1965 is a less than clean LMS Class 4 2-6-4T No 42259, from 66D Greenock, on a Glasgow train. For many years there were a numerical batch of these locos based at 66D, Nos 42258-42266, the last of which was gone by July 1966. (D.Webster)

102) Fresh from overhaul at Doncaster Works LNER A3 Class 4-6-2 No 60035 *Windsor Lad*, of 64B Haymarket, steams past the shed at St.Margarets and heads towards Edinburgh (Waverley) with the empty stock of a down express on a sunny day in 1960. *Windsor Lad*, named after one of the most famous racehorses of all time, was one of the first members of the A3's to be withdrawn, in September 1961. (N.E.Preedy)

103) Flat-roofed dwellings and a converted nissen hut in the suburbs of Edinburgh provide a backdrop in this picture as taken at Craigentinny on 24th February 1962. Deputising for a failed diesel, possibly a 'Deltic', LNER A3 Class 4-6-2 No 60082 *Neil Gow*, a resident of 52B Heaton, leaves a trail of white smoke as it passes Craigentinny South signalbox with the *Queen of Scots* Pullman express. (D.K.Jones)

104) After arrival at Tayport, on the southern bank of the Tay, from Dundee Tay Bridge, all trains had to be drawn forward clear of the convergence of the two tracks through the station. The loco then ran round the train, propelled it out towards the south and back into the other platform ready for the return journey. Performing these manouvres on 24th August 1963 is LNER Bl Class 4-6-0 No 61180 (62B Dundee Tay Bridge). (A.F.Nisbet)

105) A large billboard in the background extolls the virtues of drinking McEwan's Export and smoking Gold Leaf tobacco (both of which are frowned upon by some sections of society today) as a filthy BR Class 5 4-6-0 No 73078, from 65A Eastfield (Glasgow), steams past a diesel shunter and enters Perth (General) in pouring rain on 11th August 1963 with an express working. (D.K.Jones)

106) Countless passengers over the years must have traversed this platform at Heads of Ayr station on their way to and from the holiday camp at Butlins prior to the introduction of the family car. On 23rd June 1962 only a few passengers can he seen as LMS Class 5 4-6-0 No 45486, allocated to 67C Ayr, prepares to depart with the 9.20am express to Glasgow. By 1968 the motor car had won the battle and the station closed. (F.Hornby)

107) The bluffs on which Edinburgh Castle is built tower above the serene Princes Street gardens between which lies the quadruped main line to Glasgow and Aberdeen. Without the various overbridges like the one in the distance access to and from the gardens to the castle would be somewhat restricted. On a summer's day in 1960 LNER Al Class 4-6-2 No 60159 *Bonnie Dundee* (64B Haymarket) powers the up *Queen of Scots*. (D.K.Jones)

108) Another venue for the SLS/RCTS 'Scottish Railtour' of 1960 is at Fortrose, on the former Highland Railway branch from Muir of Ord which closed to normal passenger traffic in 1951, along with the associated stations at Redcastle, Allangrange, Munlochy and Avoch. On duty on 14th June 1960 with the special at Fortrose is former Caledonian Railway Class 3F 0-6-0 No 57594, from 60A Inverness. (F.Hornby)

(09) Judging by the looks of the signal gantry in the foreground it has been stripped of a number of its signals leaving just two, an upper and lower quadrant, the former in the off position showing a clear road ahead at Alyth Junction station. A long term resident of 61B Ferryhill (Aberdeen), LMS Class 5 4-6-0 No 44703 arrives with the 17.30 hrs Aberdeen to Perth stopping train on 8th June 1965. (K.L.Seal)

(10) Stranraer Town station looking west on 23rd June 1962. Blowing off steam and working tender-first, LMS Class 5 4-6-0 No 44995 from Dumfries shed, shunts the stock of a joint SLS/RCTS special in the foreground. To the left of the picture behind the coaching stock and goods wagons is Stranraer depot where the outline of an unidentified BR *Clan* Class 4-6-2 can just be made out. (F.Hornby)

111) Bleak and spartan hills are the hallmark of much of the scenery on the long defunct Waverley route between Carlisle and Edinburgh. At an unknown location on the line LNER BI Class 4-6-0 No 61221 *Sir Alexander Erskine-Hill*, of 64B Haymarket, clatters along with a five coach local passenger on 4th June 1960. No 61221 ended its days at 62B Dundee Tay Bridge being taken out of traffic in March 1965. (D.K.Jones)

112) As a result of the infamous 'Beeching Report' many stations which ran rival and duplicate services from major cities lost the right to run trains. One famous station which closed down was at Edinburgh (Princes Street). On 28th June 1965 LMS Class 5 4-6-0 No 44952, from 66E Carstairs, emerges from within the dark confines and out into the bright sunshine and heads for home with an express. (H.N.James)

13) The wooded copse in the background enjoys late summer sunshine on 5th September 1963 as one of Balornock's (65B St.Rollox) Caprotti BR Class 5 4-6-0's No 73146 passes the Magdalen Green in Dundee's western suburbs with an afternoon service from Dundee (West) to Glasgow (Buchanan Street). No 73146 had spells at 65A Eastfield (Glasgow) and 66B Motherwell before being withdrawn from active service in May 1967. (A.F.Nisbet)

14) We take our leave of the Scottish section of the album with a photograph of one of the most famous locomotives which worked in Scotland. Bright sunshine envelopes the station scene at Aberdeen on 2nd September 1966. LNER A2 Class 4-6-2 No 60532 *Blue Peter*, sporting a 61B Ferryhill (Aberdeen) shedplate, gingerly backs onto the carriages forming the 13.30 hrs express to Glasgow (Buchanan Street). (N.E.Preedy)

CHAPTER FIVE - SOUTHERN REGION

115) Looking in pristine external condition SR Rebuilt *West Country* Class 4-6-2 No 34014 *Budleigh Salterton*, from 75A Brighton, emerges from Southampton Tunnel and draws into the Central station with the daily Brighton to Plymouth through cross-country service on 23rd July 1963. Two months later and *Budleigh Salterton* found itself transferred to 70E Salisbury a depot it was destined to die at in March 1965. (N.E.Freedy)

16) A rain-drenched scene at Ventnor station on the Isle of Wight on 25th September 1965, at the end of the tourist season. Almost out of sight on the lattice post a signal is raised to allow for the departure of SR 02 Class 0-4-4T No 24 *Calbourne*, of 70H Ryde, on a local passenger to Shanklin, Brading and Ryde (Pier). The connection through the tunnel from Ventnor to Shanklin was severed in 1966. (Alan Jones)

17) A busy situation on the approaches to Portsmouth Harbour station on a gloomy day in 1960. Almost out of sight in the left of the frame is an unidentified Bulleid Pacific, whilst in the centre of the picture SR Rebuilt *Merchant Navy* Class 4-6-2 No 35006 *Peninsular & Oriental S.N. Co.*, from 72B Salisbury, steams in with an express. In a dead road by the platform is SR S15 Class 4-6-0 No 30497 (70B Feltham) on an excursion. (D.K.Jones)

118) A mighty Pacific is relegated to a menial duty on 28th August 1964. Having negotiated the road crossing in the distance SR Rebuilt *Battle of Britain* Class 4-6-2 No 34059 *Sir Archibald Sinclair*, another inmate of 70E Salisbury, has come to a stand with a local passenger working at Pinhoe, on the outskirts of Exeter. Withdrawn from service from Salisbury shed in May 1966, No 34059 is preserved on the Bluebell. (Alan Jones)

119) In years gone by the shedcode of 83D would have meant an allocation to Laira (Plymouth), but by early 1965 it was the designated code for Exmouth Junction (once 72A). One of its remaining inhabitants, GWR 5700 Class 0-6-0PT No 4666 is admired at Sidmouth Junction on 28th February 1965 whilst in charge of the LCGB inspired 'East Devon Rail Tour'. It was condemned from Exmouth Junction four months later. (D.Webster)

120) A raised signal clears a path for SR Maunsell N Class 2-6-0 No 31811, from 70C Guildford, which has shut off steam for the stop at Reigate in October 1964. No 31811 is hauling a Redhill to Reading passenger train. Once of 73A Stewarts Lane, No 31811 was rendered surplus to requirements in May 1959 and despatched to Guildford where it spent the remainder of its working life. Withdrawal came in July 1965. (A.C.Ingram)

121) As has been clearly observed through the pages of this and other albums many steam locomotives were employed in atrocious external conditions during the sixties, but when members of the railway hierarchy were about it appears to be a different story. An immaculate SR 700 Class 0-6-0 No 30317, from 72A Exmouth Junction, is at Barnstaple Junction on 29th June 1960 with an 'inspectors' train. (N.L.Browne)

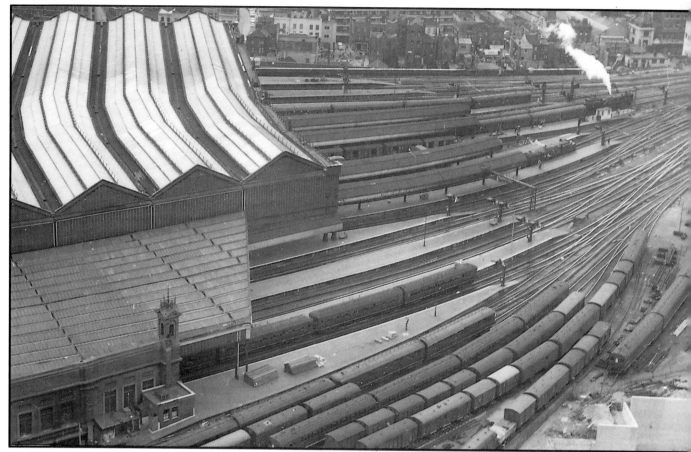

122) The photographer must have a head for heights to take this panoramic photograph of Waterloo station from the 'Shell' building in the heart of London. The different styles of roof structure can clearly be seen as can the huge amount of space required for this vast station. Two Bulleid Pacifics can be seen as are ''2-BIL'' E.M.U.'s on Windsor line semi-fasts in the foreground on 18th May 1963. (F.Hornby)

123) A garage-cum-scrapyard occupies a section of the station yard at Darking Town on 17th August 1963 (the vehicles on show would probably be worth a fortune today). SR U Class 2-6-0 No 31625, from 70C Guildford, passes the diminutive signalbox at the end of the platform with the 12.47pm cross-country passenger from Reading (Southern) to Redhill. Withdrawn in January 1964 it was saved eventually by the Mid-Hants Railway. (A.F.Nisbet)

124) A dull, overcast day at Yeovil Pen Mill station on 9th May 1963, where at one time travellers could change for Taunton and Exeter as proudly proclaimed on the board in the left of this picture. BR Class 3 2-6-2T No 82044, allocated to 83B Taunton, has the luxury of two platforms to stand between after arriving on the 6.45pm from Taunton. This engine ended its days based on the Somerset & Dorset in 1965. (J.Schatz)

125) A large crane and a modern tower-block dominate the skyline near to Southampton on 26th August 1963. SR Rebuilt *West Country* Class 4-6-2 No 34097 *Holsworthy*, a resident of 71A Eastleigh since May 1962, crosses Redbridge Causeway and approaches Totton with a Bournemouth line express. Condemned in April 1966, *Holsworthy* languished in store for a while before being towed to Cashmores, Newport for scrapping. (T.R.Amos)

126) Constructed by British Railways at the end of 1948, SR Unrebuilt *Battle of Britain* Class 4-6-2 No 34086 *219 Squadron*, one of a large number of similar locomotives based at 72A Exmouth Junction, is in a neglected state as it approaches Yeovil Junction with a Waterloo to Exeter express on 25th July 1963. When *219 Squadron* was withdrawn from 70D Eastleigh in June 1966 it had had a working life of less than 18 years. (N.E.Preedy)

127) With its bunker well stocked with coal supplies and apparently refreshed with water from the platform column SR E4 Class 0-6-0T No 32512 is ready to depart from Steyning station with a local passenger train bound for Horsham on 2nd March 1961. This former London Brighton & South Coast station demised during 1966 outliving No 32512 by some five years. The latter was cut up at Ashford Works in July 1961. (D.K.Jones)

28) If a SR *Merchant Navy* Class 4-6-2 were to appear at Waterloo nowadays it is highly unlikely that it would be ignored by all and sundry on the platform, but at mid-day on 4th October 1963 this is exactly what happened. No 35028 *Clan Line*, from the near- at-hand depot at 70A Nine Elms, is taking a breather at Waterloo after a fast run from Bournemouth with a down express. (A.F.Nisbet)

29) At a number of locations within the Southern Region there were little enclaves which employed former Great Western steam power. One which comes to mind is the shed at Folkestone which housed a number of GWR 5700 Class 0-6-0 Pannier Tanks for banking duties. Weymouth is another venue where similar engines fussed in and around the docks. On duty at Weymouth Quay on 19th August 1962 is No 7782 (71G Weymouth). (N.E.Preedy)

130) The footplate crew pass the time of day as their mount accepts a drink at Brockenhurst on 15th May 1964. SR M7 Class 0-4-4T No 30053, from 70F Bournemouth (minus shedplate), has not long arrived from Lymington Pier with a push and pull set. Although condemned a few days later No 30053 was immediately earmarked for preservation though it was laid up in store for some three years before being overhauled at Eastleigh. (A.F.Nisbet)

131) Despite the widespread electrification of the main lines in Kent during the late fifties the railway town of Ashford retained active links with steam until the closure of its shed in October 1963. 73H Dover based Light Pacific, SR Unrebuilt *Battle of Britain* Class 4-6-2 No 34083 *605 Squadron* pays a visit to Ashford station in the summer of 1960 with a Dover (Priory) express. (A.C.Ingram)

132) A timeless scene on the Isle of Wight which was to remain relatively undisturbed for a further three years or so. A member from each of the footplate crews pass the time of day at Ryde (Pierhead) on 7th July 1963. On the left SR O2 Class 0-4-4T No 16 *Ventnor* (70H Ryde) is in charge of the 1.25pm to Ventnor and on the right sister loco No 27 *Merstone* (70H Ryde) waits with the 1.30pm to Newport and Cowes. (J.Schatz)

133) High summer at Basingstoke on 1st September 1962. The junction for Reading is set and the signal pulled into the 'off' position in readiness for the departure of highly polished GWR *Hall* Class 4-6-0 No 6929 *Whorlton Hall*, from 84C Banbury, which is powering a Bournemouth to Sheffield holiday express. Despite its fine condition No 6929 had just over one year left to live being withdrawn in October 1963. (J.Schatz)

134) Looking well overdue for a visit to workshops SR Bulleid Unrebuilt *Battle of Britain* Class 4-6-2 No 34070 *Manston*, allocated to 73H Dover, raises the echoes as it climbs past woodland on the 1 in 100 gradient out of Maidstone with a heavy boat train in August 1960. From May 1961 to November 1961 *Manston* had a brief association with 73F Ashford before being drafted hundreds of miles away to 72A Exmouth Junction. (Brian Coates)

135) Sporting its virtually brand new shedcode of 70E, Salisbury based SR Rebuilt *Merchant Navy* Class 4-6-2 No 35007 *Aberdeen Commonwealth* lifts a lengthy Exeter to Waterloo express out of Yeovil Junction on 16th September 1963. Constructed at Eastleigh Works in June 1942, *Aberdeen Commonwealth* was originally allocated the number 21C-7. It was rebuilt during May 1958 and withdrawn in July 1967 from 70A Nine Elms. (N.E.Preedy)

136) SR Unrebuilt *West Country* Class 4-6-2 No 34011 *Tavistock*, from 72A Exmouth Junction, gingerly eases its short train over the narrow curving trestle bridge which crosses the river Tawe at Barnstaple on 6th May 1963. *Tavistock* is in charge of the 8.58am passenger from Ilfracombe to Salisbury. The link from Barnstaple to Ilfracombe was severed in 1970, seven years after the demise of *Tavistock*. (J.Schatz)

137) We complete this pictorial quartet of Bulleid Light Pacifics with a photograph of SR Rebuilt *Battle of Britain* Class 4-6-2 No 34077 *603 Squadron*, which has been neglected by the cleaning staff at 70A Nine Elms. It is seen here accelerating through Vauxhall station with a down West of England express on 4th July 1964. For some obscure reason No 34077 was transferred to 70B Feltham in September 1964. (F.Hornby)

138) The tranquility of a rural station is disturbed briefly by the presence of a local passenger train. Presumably on loan to Wadebridge shed, GWR 4500 Class 2-6-2T No 4574 heads a Bodmin line stopper on an unknown day in 1961. Allocated to Truro since January 1957 No 4574 moved on to 83A Newton Abbot in September 1961. One further transfer in August 1962 took it to a final home at 83D Laira (Plymouth). (D.K.Jones)

139) The rusting track in the left of this picture along with the sprouting of weeds are a sign of the times at Hawkhurst station on 3rd June 1961. There is only one week to go before this small terminus on the branch from Paddock Wood is closed and the signalman on the steps of his box may well be pondering his future. In the foreground is SR H Class 0-4-4T No 31177, from Tonbridge shed on a local passenger. (F.Hornby)

40) Bright summer sunshine reflects off the boiler of BR Class 4 2-6-0 No 76011, from 71A Eastleigh, as it waits patiently at Salisbury on 27th July 1963 with a Swansea to Brockenhurst express. Based at Eastleigh in January 1957, No 76011 was moved to 72C Yeovil from September 1958 to January 1959 when it returned to the former depot. A final transfer in October 1965 took it to 70F Bournemouth. (B.W.L.Brooksbank)

41) SR Rebuilt *Merchant Navy* Class 4-6-2 No 35010 *Blue Star*, allocated to 70F Bournemouth, emerges from the shadows cast by the wooded terrain near to its home and into bright sunlight with an unidentified express on 15th July 1966. The writing was on the wall for this 1942 built Pacific with condemnation only two short months away. The signs are already in place with a missing shedcode and home-made numberplate. (D.K.Jones)

142) Signals of various designs, speed restriction signs and cross-overs abound at Redhill station on 11th August 1962. Almost at the end of its career SR Ul Class 2-6-0 No 31906, from 75C Norwood Junction, has been seconded to head a lengthy Brighton to Birmingham express which consists of LMR stock. Withdrawn from regular traffic in December 1962, No 31906 was stored at 75C and 71A Eastleigh for some time. (F.Hornby)

143) For countless years the line from Swanage to Wareham (with the connection to the former LSWR main line from Bournemouth to Weymouth) was worked by the sturdy SR M7 Class 0-4-4 Tanks. In the sixties these erstwhile engines were superseded by more modern examples of motive power like BR Class 4 2-6-4T No 80032 (70F Bournemouth) seen leaving Swanage with the 12.25pm to Wareham on 8th August 1966. (T.R.Amos)

144) On 14th August 1960 'The Greyhound' railtour, organised by the Railway Correspondence and Travel Society, pauses at Yeovil Junction in Somerset on its way from Salisbury to Weymouth, giving the fireman a chance to shovel some coal forward in the tender. The stop also gives the photographers an opportunity to record SR T9 Class 4-4-0 No 30718, from 72A Exmouth Junction (minus shedplate). (Peter Hay)

145) The 'Big Freeze' of 1962-1963 commenced on or around the 23rd December 1962 and for those readers who were to young to remember those far off days this picture typifies the wintry conditions. SR Unrebuilt *Battle of Britain* Class 4-6-2 No 34057 *Biggin Hill* (75A Brighton) battles its way through a blizzard at Warnham station with the 5.13am London Bridge to Brighton express on 27th December 1962. (A.C.Ingram)

146) The tracks, sidings and stations at Gloucester (Central and Eastgate) were basically run as a joint venture by the Great Western and Midland Railway and this picture typifies the mixture of both with Midland signals and signalbox in view together with a GWR locomotive. 5100 Class 2-6-2T No 4100, based at nearby 85B Horton Road, passes Tramway Junction with the Cheltenham portion of an express on 4th August 1964. (J.K.Carter)

147) In its heyday Shrewsbury was a major crossroad for lines which radiated in many directions and it hosted locomotives of BR, GWR and LMS origins. Passengers and spotters alike intermingle on various platforms on 16th June 1961. The centrepiece of this picture is devoted to LMS Class 2 2-6-2T No 41231, from 84H Wellington, seen blowing off surplus steam whilst in charge of a local passenger. (D.K.Jones)

148) Usually the shed staff at 85A Worcester took great pride in keeping its fleet of GWR *Castle* Class 4-6-0's in a high state of cleanliness, but this example is far from clean. No 7002 *Devizes Castle* enters Oxford station with the up *Cathedrals Express* on its way from Worcester to Paddington on 21st May 1960. Even the nameboard of this titled train is a 'home-made' effort, along with the chalked reporting number. (N.L.Browne)

149) A usurper on the Western Region. Sporting the excursion headcode of 1X86, begrimed LMS *Jubilee* Class 4-6-0 No 45660 *Rooke*, an inhabitant of 6D Shrewsbury, slows for the curve at West Wycombe with a twelve coach schoolboy International Football special in May 1964. During the following month *Rooke* was transferred to 6A Chester, but within a few short weeks it was despatched to the NER at 55A Leeds (Holbeck). (D.Coles)

150) Newly reallocated to 87A Neath, from 87E Landore (Swansea) following the closure of the latter for rebuilding into a diesel depot, GWR *Castle* Class 4-6-0 No 5062 *Earl of Shaftesbury* (with white painted buffers) is seen at Paddington station on 7th July 1961 prior to departure to Swansea with the down *Pembroke Coast Express*. There was only a limited future for No 5062, withdrawn from 87F Llanelly in August 1962. (D.K.Jones)

151) A mass of scaffolding points to the fact that a hotel style of premise is being refurbished in front of Barmouth station. On possibly one of its last duties at 89C Machynlleth before being transferred to 6H Bangor, BR Class 2 2-6-0 No 78002 prepares to depart with the 4.15pm local passenger to Dolgellau on 12th June 1963. No 78002 ended its days in Preston, being based at 10D Lostock Hall. (F.Hornby)

152) A wet day in the Welsh Valleys on 5th June 1964. Below us, to the left, we can espy some signals which guard the approach to Quakers Yard Low Level, on the line from Merthyr to Pontypridd (joint Great Western/Taff Vale). White smoke and steam fill the atmosphere as GWR 5700 Class 0-6-0PT No 3708, from 86G Pontypool Road, rattles into Quakers Yard High Level (GWR) with a two coach local from Neath to Pontypool. (W.Potter)

153) Steam to the rescue at Tyseley on 23rd August 1962. Based at the nearby depot 84E, GWR 5100 Class 2-6-2T No 4155 has been commandeered to assist the ailing prototype *Western* Type 4 diesel-hydraulic C-C No D1000 *Western Enterprise* for haulage to Birmingham (Snow Hill) with a Paddington to Birkenhead express. In the top left of the picture we can just make out the junction to Stratford-on-Avon. (Mike Wood)

154) Special traffic on the former Somerset & Dorset Railway on 4th April 1965. With steam to spare LMS Class 8F 2-8-0 No 48309, from 82F Bath Green Park, clears its cylinder cocks whilst at a standstill at Shepton Mallet. No 48309 is in charge of the LCGB 'The Wessex Downsman Rail Tour'. Although an LMS loco No 48309 spent much of its life on the Western Region including 87K Swansea (Victoria) and 87F Llanelly. (D.Webster)

155) Glandyfi station (Cambrian Railways) looking north towards Dovey Junction in September 1961. A wooden posted signal bows downwards to allow GWR 4300 Class 2-6-0 No 6368, from far off 85A Worcester, to depart with a holiday express from the Midlands to Aberystwyth. No 6368 is working 'wrong line' which points to the fact that it might be a Sunday. Note the elderly camping coach in a siding to the right. (N.L.Browne)

156) A photograph of GWR 4500 Class 2-6-2T No 5525 (83B Taunton) at work on the West Somerset line on 4th July 1961 shortly before a transfer to 83A Newton Abbot. It is working bunker-first on a Minehead to Taunton passenger train at Watchet. Note the main station building at right angles to the track. Watchet station opened in March 1862 and closed to passengers in January 1971. It is now privately preserved. (N.L.Browne)

157) One of the few lines which was spared from the Beeching Axe in mid-Wales is that from Shrewsbury to Aberystwyth via Welshpool, Newtown, Talerddig, Cemmaes Road and Dovey Junction. Many of the stations along this route did in fact close. One which survived is at Caersws, a one time junction of a branch to Van Garth Road. In charge of a passenger train on 11th July 1964 is LMS Class 2 2-6-0 No 46521. (D.K.Jones)

158) A wet and miserable looking day at Oxford on 21st May 1960. Parcels and packages are piled onto a trolley on the platform which is occupied by a less than clean 84C Banbury based GWR 5100 Class 2-6-2T No 4154 which is hauling a northbound three coach non- corridor set. Primarily based at sheds in the Midlands from the late fifties onwards, No 4154 had a brief sojourn at 83A Newton Abbot early in 1960. (N.L.Browne)

59) An almost deserted scene within the splendid confines of Birmingham (Snow Hill) station on 26th May 1963. Occupying platforms 5 and 6 is an excursion, the 9.10am to Birkenhead (Woodside). Entrusted with the task of hauling this express is GWR *Modified Hall* Class 4-6-0 No 7918 *Rhose Wood Hall,* from 84E Tyseley, a shed it was to die at under the changed code of 2A in February 1965. (J.Schatz)

60) By January 1957 many inroads had been made into the GWR 4300 Class 2-6-0's by withdrawals, thus by this date No 5306 was the first numerical member of the 5300 series to still be in service. On 10th September 1961 it was still in full employment, based at 86G Pontypool Road, and being utilised by the RCTS to haul a rail special. The location of this picture is Cheltenham (St.James). (D.Webster)

161) For many years, at least until September 1963, the shed at Shrewsbury had a number of GWR *County* Class 4-6-0's on its books, these being Nos 1002/3/8/13/14/16/17/19/22/23/25-27, though not all at the same time. One of them, No 1017 *County of Hereford*, steams beneath a signal gantry at Shrewsbury station and heads towards Birkenhead with the 4.22pm local passenger on 21st October 1962. (J.Schatz)

162) The infamous Lickey Incline, between Blackwell and Bromsgrove came under, the auspices of both the London Midland and Western Regions at different times following nationalisation in 1948. On 25th August 1962 it was firmly in the grip of the Western with its destiny controlled from Gloucester. A filthy LMS *Jubilee* Class 4-6-0 No 45725 *Repulse* (41A Sheffield - Darnall) climbs the bank with a Bristol-Sheffield express. (R.Picton)

53) There is more than enough cover for would be passengers at Severn Tunnel station as can be seen from the enclosed footbridge and extended canopy over the nearest platform. Steam leaks from various joints of GWR 5100 Class 2-6-2T No 5188, an inhabitant of the massive shed at 86A Newport (Ebbw Junction), which is waiting to depart with a Chepstow bound three coach local passenger on 24th April 1962. (R.Picton)

54) Another local passenger working, this time at Swindon station on 12th August 1962. GWR *Modified Hall* Class 4-6-0 No 7926 *Willey Hall*, from 85B Gloucester (Horton Road), powers a Gloucester to Paddington stopping train. The following month *Willey Hall* was drafted to 85A Worcester. During its final year of active service, 1964, No 7926 was based at 81D Reading, 82C Swindon and finally back to Horton Road. (N.L.Browne)

165) The barren hill in the distance is in direct contrast to the lush vegetation in the foreground of this picture. Puffs of white smoke trail behind GWR 5100 Class 2-6-2T No 4110, allocated to 87A Neath, as it departs from Quakers Yard High Level and trundles over the viaduct with a Pontypool Road to Neath train on 13th June 1964. This service was withdrawn the following day. Another Beeching 'triumph'. (W.Potter)

166) Another view of a Neath to Pontypool Road service, in happier times, though the iron overbridge could do with a lick of paint. Smoke and steam swirl around in the wind at Aberdare (High Level) on 21st August 1961 as GWR 5700 Class 0-6-0PT No 8707 makes ready to depart with the 10.30am from Neath (General). A long time favourite of 86G Pontypool Road, No 8707 was withdrawn from there in July 1964. (J.M.Tolson)

57) We move from the heart of the Welsh Valleys with its slower pace of life to the hustle and bustle of the city of London. On 6th May 1961 GWR 5700 Class 0-6-0PT No 9710, fitted with condensing apparatus, chugs past a signalbox at Westbourne Park and heads for Paddington with the empty coaching stock it has hauled from Old Oak Common. No 9710 spent most, if not all, of its working life based at 81A Old Oak. (F.Hornby)

58) The little Midland Railway signalbox at Standish Junction, near Gloucester, stands guard over crucial pointwork during the summer of 1962. GWR *Castle* Class 4-6-0 No 7024 *Powis* Castle, from 84A Wolverhampton (Stafford Road), negotiates the points as it moves from Midland to Western Region tracks with a Saturdays Only relief express from Penzance to Wolverhampton (Low Level) - designated train reporting No H31. (F.A.Bridgman)

169) The authorities at Reading (General) station must have been unaware of the group of lads who were dangling their legs over the platform in the left of this picture or they surely would have taken some action to prevent this dangerous practice? Moving away from this problem the camera lens have been trained on GWR *Castle* Class 4-6-0 No 7027 *Thornbury Castle* with a Paddington-Worcester express on 16th June 1962. (D.Webster)

170) High summer on the Somerset & Dorset. The peace and quiet of this amiable line is disturbed by the twin exhausts of BR Class 4 4-6-0 No 75009 (82G Templecombe) and BR Class 9F 2-10-0 No 92001, from 82F Bath Green Park and equipped with a double chimney, as they power the up *Pines Express* through Midford on 25th August 1962. In September 1962 this train was given a new route, via Birmingham (Snow Hill) and Oxford. (N.E.Preedy)

1) Possibly deputising for a GWR *King* Class 4-6-0, GWR *Castle* Class 4-6-0 No 7014 *Caerhays Castle*, of 84A Wolverhampton (Stafford Road), emerges from the short tunnel from Hockley with the 11.45am express from Birkenhead (Woodside) to Paddington (VO7) on 1st July 1962. Constructed by British Railways in June 1949 at Swindon, *Caerhays Castle* later acquired a double chimney - March 1959. (J.Schatz)

2) Using the thronging crowd as evidence, this may well be the last day of normal passenger services on the Fairford Branch. Having just run round its stock, a cleaned and polished GWR 5700 Class 0-6-0PT No 9654 (81F Oxford) draws the empty stock of the 2.25pm local passenger to Oxford into the single platform at Fairford on 16th June 1962. No 9654 was with us no more after October 1964, withdrawn from 81F. (J.M.Tolson)

173) Row upon row of gaunt and forbidding dwelling places look down upon the former Great Western main line from Paddington, at Westbourne Park on 6th May 1961. Having brought an up express into the terminus GWR *Castle* Class 4-6-0 No 5093 *Upton Castle* is in a secondary role as it trails behind its stock which is being hauled to Old Oak sidings by a Pannier Tank. *Upton Castle* is returning to its base at 81A Old Oak Common. (F.Hornby)

174) GWR *Hall* Class 4-6-0 No 6943 *Farnley Hall*, from 85B Gloucester (Horton Road), leaves Gloucester with 1Z73, a relief to the *Cornishman*, from Wolverhampton (Low Level) to Penzance on 3rd August 1963. Once of 86C Cardiff (Canton), *Farnley Hall* had been at Horton Road since February 1962. It was to die there in December 1963. The location where No 6943 is now forms part of the inner city ring road at Gloucester. (N.E.Preedy)